JSON

Main principals

By David. V.

Contents

Introduction

JSON is a very useful framework when it comes to the development of software apps. There is an increased need for transfer of data in a format which can be read by humans. Also, people need creating websites which will have the ability to update data live. JSON can help you in this. This book guides you step by step on how to do it.

Chapter 1- A Brief Overview of JSON

JSON is an open standard which is used for the purpose of transmission of data objects in human-readable text. It forms the primary data format which is used for asynchronous browser/server communication and this has replaced XML. The standard was derived from JavaScript, but it is a language-independent data format. Code for generation and parsing of JSON data is always available in various types of programming languages.

The reason for the tremendous growth in JSON is the need for a real-time, server-to-browser communication without the need to use browser plugins such as Java applets or Flash.

Chapter 2- Syntax

The syntax used in JSON is seen as a subset of the syntax used in JavaScript. It is made up of the following:
• Representation of data is done in name/value pairs.
• Curly braces for holding objects and each name has to be followed by ':'(colon), the name/value pairs separated by, (comma).
• Square brackets for holding arrays and values should be separated by, (comma).
Consider the simple example which is given below:

```
{

  "book": [

    {
      "id":"01",
      "language": "Android",
      "edition": "fourth",
      "author": "Joel John"
    },


    {
      "id":"07",
      "language": "C++",
      "edition": "third",
      "author": "Mercy Joel"
    }

  ]
}
```

JSON supports the data structures given below:
• **Collection of name/value pairs-** this is a data structure which is supported by different programming languages.
• **Ordered list of values- this is made up of** list, array, vector or sequence, and others.

Chapter 3- Data Types in JSON

Let us discuss the data types which are supported in JSON.

Number

This refers to a double-precision floating point format used in JavaScript, and it is determined by its implementation. Hexadecimal and Octal formats are not supported in JSON. The following are the numbers which are supported in JSON:

- Integer- Digits 1-9, 0 and positive or negative
- Fraction- such as .5, .3, .9
- Exponents- such as e, e+, e-, E, E+, E-

These are defined using the syntax given below:

var json-object-name = { string : number_value, ...}

Consider the example given below:

var student = {marks: 57}

String

This is made up of zero or more Unicode characters having a backslash as the escape sequence. A single character string represents a Character, that is, a string having a length of 1.

Consider the table given below, which shows the available string types:

•	"	-double quotation
•	\	-reverse solidus
•	/	-Solidus
•	b	-Backspace
•	f	-form feed
•	n	-new line
•	r	-carriage return
•	t	-horizontal tab
•	u	-four hexadecimal digits

They use the syntax given below:

var json-object-name = { string : "string value", ...}

Below is an example of a String data type:

var object = {name: 'John'}

Boolean

This takes either *"true"* or *"false"* values. It takes the syntax given below:

var json-object-name = { string : true/false, ...}

Consider the cxample given below:

var object = {name: 'John', marks: 57, distinction: true}

Array

This represents an ordered collection of values. Square brackets are used for the purpose of enclosing the values of an array. This means that the array has to begin with a square bracket, and also end with a square bracket. The values inside the array have to be separated by use of a comma. The indexing can be started from either 0 or 1.

Arrays take the syntax given below:

[value, ...]

Consider the array given below, which shows an array having numerous values:

```
{
  "books": [
    { "language":"Android" , "edition":"third" },
    { "language":"C++" , "lastName":"fifth" },
    { "language":"Java" , "lastName":"second" }
  ]
}
```

Object

This represents an unordered set of pairs of values. The objects have to be enclosed within curly braces, which means that they have to start with a curly brace "{"and end with a curly brace "}." Each name in the object has to be followed by a colon (:), and the names themselves are separated by use of a comma. The keys used have to be strings, and each has to be unique.

The following syntax is used for definition of objects:

{ string : value, ...}

Consider the example given below:
```
{
  "id": "022B",
  "language": "JAVA",
  "price": 600,
}
```

Whitespace

This can be inserted between any pair of the tokens. It is added when one wants to make their code to be more readable. It takes the syntax given below:

{string:" ",....}

Consider the example given below:

var p = " john";

var q = " joel"

null

This represents an empty type. It takes the following syntax:
Consider the example given below:

var j = null;

```
if(j == 1){
  document.write("<h1>value of j is 1</h1>");
}
else{
  document.write("<h1>value is null</h1>");
}
```

JSON Value

This includes the following:
• array
• boolean
• number (integer or floating point)
• string
• null
• object
It takes the syntax given below:

String | Number | Object | Array | TRUE | FALSE | NULL

Consider the example given below:

var p = 1;
var q = "john";
var r = null;

Chapter 4- Objects in JSON

JavaScript can be used for the purpose of creating JSON objects. There are various ways how this can be done. Let us discuss these ways.

Creating an empty object:

var JSONObj = {};

Creating a new object:

var JSONObject = new Object();

Using **bookname** to create an object with the value in string:

var JSONObject = { "bookname ":"C++ INTRODUCTORY BOOK", "price":600 };

JSON can be used for the creation of objects in JavaScript. This is shown below:

```
<html>
 <head>
  <title>Creating a JSON Object with
JavaScript</title>

  <script language = "javascript" >

    var JSONObject = { "name" : "mysite.com", "year"
: 2007 };

    document.write("<h1>JSON with JavaScript
example</h1>");
    document.write("<br>");
    document.write("<h3>Website Name =
"+JSONObject.name+"</h3>");

    document.write("<h3>Year =
"+JSONObject.year+"</h3>");

  </script>

 </head>

 <body>
 </body>
```

```
</html>
```
You can save the above program, and then open it in your browser. It should give you the following output:

Website Name = mysite.com

Year = 2007

Creating Array Objects

JSON can be used for creation of an array object in JavaScript. Consider the example given below which shows how this can be done:

```html
<html>
  <head>
    <title>Creating an array object in javascript by use of JSON</title>

    <script language = "javascript" >

      document.writeln("<h2>A JSON array object</h2>");

      var books = { "C" : [
        { "Name" : "C Made Simple", "price" : 800 },

        { "Name" : "Guide to C", "price" : 500 }],

        "Java" : [
          { "Name" : "Java for Beginners", "price" : 1200 },
          { "Name" : "Java in Depth", "price" : 1400 }]
      }

      var j = 0
      document.writeln("<table border = '2'><tr>");

      for(j = 0;j<books.C.length;j++){
        document.writeln("<td>");
```

```
        document.writeln("<table border = '1' width =
100 >");
        document.writeln("<tr><td><b>Name</b></td
><td width = 50>" + books.C[i].Name+"</td></tr>");

        document.writeln("<tr><td><b>Price</b></td
><td width = 50>" + books.C[i].price +"</td></tr>");

        document.writeln("</table>");
        document.writeln("</td>");
    }

    for(i = 0;i<books.Java.length;i++){

        document.writeln("<td>");
        document.writeln("<table border = '1' width =
100 >");
        document.writeln("<tr><td><b>Name</b></td
><td width = 50>" +
books.Java[i].Name+"</td></tr>");

        document.writeln("<tr><td><b>Price</b></td
><td width = 50>" +
books.Java[i].price+"</td></tr>");

        document.writeln("</table>");
        document.writeln("</td>");
    }

    document.writeln("</tr></table>");

  </script>

 </head>

 <body>
 </body>

</html>
```

Chapter 5- Schema

This is a specification which is used for definition of the structure of JSON data. When used, it can describe the structure of the data format which is currently being used. One is provided with a complete structural validation, which is very important when it comes to automated testing. It is also good for validation of data which has been supplied by clients.

Libraries for JSON Schema validation

There are different validates which are currently available for the various programming languages. These include the following:

• C	-WJElement
• Java	-json-schema-validator
• .NET	-Json.NET
• ActionScript 3	-Frigga
• Haskell	-aeson-schema
• Python	-Jsonschema
• Ruby	-autoparse ;ruby-jsonschema
• PHP	-php-json-schema. json-schema
• JavaScript	-Orderly ; JSV; json-schema; Matic; Dojo; Persevere; schema.js.

Consider the example given below:

```
{
  "$schema": "http://json-schema.org/draft-04/schema#",
  "title": "Product",
  "description": "A product catalog",
  "type": "object",

  "properties": {

    "id": {
      "description": "This is a unique identifier for the product",
```

```
    "type": "integer"
  },

  "name": {
    "description": "Name of our product",
    "type": "string"
  },

  "price": {
    "type": "number",
    "minimum": 0,
    "exclusiveMinimum": true
  }
},

  "required": ["id", "name", "price"]
}
```
There are a number of keywords which can be used during the definition of a schema. These are explained below:

• $schema- this keyword states that the schema has been written according to our draft v4 specification.

• title- this will be used for the purpose of assigning a title to a schema.

• description- this provides a little specification of your schema.

• type- this keyword defines our first constraint on the JSON data: it must be a JSON Object.

• properties- used for definition of various keys, and the value for the keys. They are the minimum and the maximum values which should be used in the JSON file.

• required- this specifies the list of properties which are required.

• minimum- this constraint is put on a value for specification of the minimum value which is acceptable.

• pattern- an instance of a string is considered to be valid if the regular expression has successfully matched the instance.

• maxLength- this is the maximum number of characters which can be accepted for a string.

Consider the example given below:

```
[
  {
    "id": 1,
    "name": "Ice sculpture",
    "price": 10.60,
  },

  {
    "id": 2,
    "name": "A blue mouse",
    "price": 19.50,
  }
]
```

Chapter 6- JSON vs. XML

These two standards represent a human readable format, and they are language independent. These can support reading, creation, and decoding in real-life situations. The following factors can be used for the sake of comparison of JSON and XML.

Verbose

When the two are compared, XML is found to be more verbose as compared to JSON. This means that on the programmers' part, writing JSON is faster that XML.

Arrays Usage

XML is used when we need describing structured data, and arrays are not included. In JSON, arrays are included.

Parsing

The "*eval*" method of JavaScript is used for the purpose of parsing JSON. When this has been applied to JSON, then the eval will describe the object which has been described. Consider the examples given below:

XML

```
<car>
 <company>Toyota</company>
 <name>Premio</name>
 <price>500000</price>
</car>
```

JSON

```
{
 "company": Toyota,
 "name": "Premio",
 "price": 500000
}
```

That is how the two standards compare to each other.

Chapter 7- Http Requests in JSON

JSON is commonly used for the purpose of reading data from a server. The same data is then displayed on a web page. This chapter will demonstrate how this can be done in easy steps. You will learn how to use XMLHttp to read JSON data.
Consider the example given below:

```
<!DOCTYPE html>
<html>
<body>
<div id="ido1"></div>

<script>
var xmlhttp = new XMLHttpRequest();
var url = "mysite.txt";
xmlhttp.onreadystatechange = function() {
  if (xmlhttp.readyState == 4 && xmlhttp.status ==
200) {
    var myArray =
JSON.parse(xmlhttp.responseText);
    myFunction(myArray);
  }
};
xmlhttp.open("GET", url, true);
xmlhttp.send();

function myFunction(array) {
  var out = "";
  var j;
  for(j = 0; j < array.length; j++) {
    out += '<a href="' + arr[i].url + '">' +
    array[j].display + '</a><br>';

  }
  document.getElementById("ido1").innerHTML =
out;
}
</script>
</body>
```

</html>

With the above example, the menu on the site *"mysite.com"* will be read and then displayed on a web page.

Creation of an Array of Objects

An array literal should be used for the purpose of declaration of an array of objects. Each object should be given two properties, that is, display and url. Consider the example given below:

```
var array = [
{
"display": "JSON Tutorial",
"url": "http://www.mysite.com/js/default.asp"
},
{
"display": "HTML Tutorial",
"url": "http://www.mysite.com/html/default.asp"
},
{
"display": "CSS Tutorial",
"url": "http://www.mysite.com/css/default.asp"
}
]
```

That is how we have created our array having the list of tutorials which we have on the site *"mysite.com."*

Creation of a JavaScript Function for displaying the Array

We need to come up with a function which will loop through the contents of the array, and then display them in an HTML links format.

Here is the example:

```
function myFunction(array) {
    var out = "";
    var j;
    for(j = 0; j < array.length; j++) {
        out += '<a href="' + array[j].url + '">' +
array[j].display + '</a><br>';
    }
```

```
    document.getElementById("ido1").innerHTML =
out;
}
```

The function *"myFunction"* can be called and *"array"* will be passed in as the argument. This is shown below:

```
<!DOCTYPE html>
<html>
<body>
<div id="ido1"></div>
<script>
var array = [
{
"display": "JSON Tutorial",
"url": "http://www.mysite.com/js/default.asp"
},
{
"display": "HTML Tutorial",
"url": "http://www.mysite.com/html/default.asp"
},
{
"display": "CSS Tutorial",
"url": "http://www.mysite.com/css/default.asp"
}
];
myFunction(array);
function myFunction(array) {
  var out = "";
  var j;
  for(j = 0; j < array.length; j++) {
    out += '<a href="' + arr[j].url + '">' +
    array[j].display + '</a><br>';
  }
  document.getElementById("ido1").innerHTML =
out;
}
</script>
</body>
</html>
```

The array literal should be put into a file named *"tutorials.txt."* Here is the file:

```
[
{
"display": "HTML Tutorial",
"url": "http://www.mysite.com/html/default.asp"
},
{
"display": "CSS Tutorial",
"url": "http://www.mysite.com/css/default.asp"
},
{
"display": "JavaScript Tutorial",
"url": "http://www.mysite.com/js/default.asp"
},
{
"display": "jQuery Tutorial",
"url": "http://www.mysite.com/jquery/default.asp"
},
{
"display": "JSON Tutorial",
"url": "http://www.mysite.com/json/default.asp"
},
{
"display": "iOS Tutorial",

"url": "http://www.mysite.com/ajax/default.asp"
},
{
"display": "SQL Tutorial",
"url": "http://www.mysite.com/sql/default.asp"
},
{
"display": "PHP Tutorial",
"url": "http://www.mysite.com/php/default.asp"
},
{
```

```
"display": "Oracle Tutorial",
"url": "http://www.mysite.com/xml/default.asp"
}
]
```

Using "XMLHttpRequest" to read the text file

Create an *"XMLHttpRequest"* which will be used for reading the text file, and then use the function *"myFunction()"* to display the value of the array. This is shown below:

```
<!DOCTYPE html>
<html>
<body>
<div id="id01"></div>
<script>
var xmlhttp = new XMLHttpRequest();
var url = "tutorials.txt";
xmlhttp.onreadystatechange = function() {
  if (xmlhttp.readyState == 4 && xmlhttp.status ==
200) {
    var array= JSON.parse(xmlhttp.responseText);
    myFunction(array);
  }
};
xmlhttp.open("GET", url, true);
xmlhttp.send();
function myFunction(array) {
  var out = "";
  var j;
  for(j = 0; j < arr.length; j++) {
    out += '<a href="' + arr[j].url + '">' +
    arr[j].display + '</a><br>';
  }
  document.getElementById("id01").innerHTML =
out;
}
</script>
</body>
</html>
```

Chapter 8- Function Files in JSON

JSON is commonly used for reading data from a web server. This data is then displayed on a web page. Function files can be used for the purpose of reading JSON data. This book will guide you on how to do this.

We need to create an example which will read data from *"mysite.js"* and then display it on a web page. This is shown in the example given below:

```
<!DOCTYPE html>
<html>
<body>
<div id="ido1"></div>
<script>
function myFunction(array) {
  var out = "";
  var j;
  for(j = 0; j<array.length; j++) {
    out += '<a href="' + array[j].url + '">' +
    array[j].display + '</a><br>';
  }
  document.getElementById("ido1").innerHTML =
out;
}
</script>
<script src="mysite.js"></script>
</body>
</html>
```

Creation of an Array of Objects

This can be done by use of an array of literals. This is shown below:

```
var array = [
{
"display": "JSON Tutorial",
"url": "http://www.mysite.com/js/default.asp"
},
{
"display": "HTML Tutorial",
```

```
"url": "http://www.mysite.com/html/default.asp"
},
{
"display": "CSS Tutorial",
"url": "http://www.mysite.com/css/default.asp"
}
]
```

The following function will loop through the contents of the array and then display the contents as links:

```
function myFunction(array) {
   var out = "";
   var j;
   for(j = 0; j < array.length; j++) {
      out += '<a href="' + array[j].url + '">' +
array[j].display + '</a><br>';
   }
   document.getElementById("id01").innerHTML =
out;
}
```

The function can then be called as follows:

```
<!DOCTYPE html>
<html>
<body>
<div id="id01"></div>
<script>
var array = [
{
"display": "JSON Tutorial",
"url": "http://www.mysite.com/js/default.asp"
},
{
"display": "HTML Tutorial",
"url": "http://www.mysite.com/html/default.asp"
},
{
"display": "CSS Tutorial",
"url": "http://www.mysite.com/css/default.asp"
}
];
```

```
myFunction(array);
function myFunction(array) {
  var out = "";
  var j;
  for(j = 0; j < array.length; j++) {
    out += '<a href="' + array[j].url + '">' +
    array[j].display + '</a><br>';
  }
  document.getElementById("ido1").innerHTML =
out;
}
</script>
</body>
</html>
```

An array literal can also be used as an argument. This can be demonstrated by calling our function by passing an array literal as the argument. This is shown below:

```
<!DOCTYPE html>
<html>
<body>
<div id="ido1"></div>
<script>
myFunction([
{
"display": "JSON Tutorial",
"url": "http://www.mysite.com/js/default.asp"
},
{
"display": "HTML Tutorial",
"url": "http://www.mysite.com/html/default.asp"
},
{
"display": "CSS Tutorial",
"url": "http://www.mysite.com/css/default.asp"
}
]);
function myFunction(array) {
  var out = "";
  var j;
```

26

```
  for(j = 0; j<arr.length; j++) {
    out += '<a href="' + array[j].url + '">' +
    array[j].display + '</a><br>';
  }
  document.getElementById("id01").innerHTML =
out;
}
</script>
</body>
</html>
```

The function call can then be put in an external function call.
This is shown below:

```
myFunction([
{
"display": "JSON Tutorial",
"url": "http://www.mysite.com/js/default.asp"
},
{
"display": "HTML Tutorial",
"url": "http://www.mysite.com/html/default.asp"
},
{
"display": "CSS Tutorial",
"url": "http://www.mysite.com/css/default.asp"
}
]);
```

The external script can be added to the page as shown below:

```
<!DOCTYPE html>
<html>
<body>
<div id="id01"></div>
<script>
function myFunction(array) {
  var out = "";
  var j;
  for(j = 0; j<array.length; j++) {
    out += '<a href="' + array[j].url + '">' +
    array[j].display + '</a><br>';
  }
```

```
    document.getElementById("ido1").innerHTML =
out;
}
</script>
<script src="mysite.js"></script>
</body>
</html>
```

Chapter 9- JSON with PHP

JSON objects can be encoded and also decoded by use of PHP programming language. However, before beginning, you should first set up your environment.

Environment

For PHP 5.2.0, the JSON extension has been bundled and compiled into PHP by default.

JSON Functions

• json_encode- this returns the JSON representation of the value.
• json_decode- for decoding a JSON string.
• json_last_error- this will return the last error which occurred.

Encoding JSON in PHP

The PHP function "json_encode()" is used for the purpose of encoding JSON in PHP. When used, the function always returns a JSON representation of the value on a success or a FALSE failure. It takes the syntax given below:

string json_encode ($value [, $options = 0])

The following parameters have been used:

• Value - this is the value which is being encoded. The function will only work with UTF-8 encoded data.
• Options - this is a bitmask which is made up of the following values JSON_UNESCAPED_SLASHES, JSON_HEX_TAG, JSON_HEX_AMP, JSON_HEX_QUOT, JSON_HEX_APOS, JSON_NUMERIC_CHECK, JSON_FORCE_OBJECT, JSON_PRETTY_PRINT.

When using PHP, an array can be converted into JSON. This is shown below:

```php
<?php
 $arr = array('p' => 1, 'q' => 2, 'r' => 3, 's' => 4, 't' => 5);
 echo json_encode($array);
?>
```

Execution of the above code will give you the following output:
{"p":1,"q":2,"r":3,"s":4,"t":5}

Conversion of PHP objects into JSON can also be done. This is shown below:

```php
<?php
 class Employee {
   public $name = "";
   public $leisure  = "";
   public $birthdate = "";
 }

 $e = new Employee();
 $e->name = "john";
 $e->leisure  = "sporting";
 $e->birthdate = date('m/d/Y h:i:s a', "8/5/1992
12:30:06 p");
 $e->birthdate = date('m/d/Y h:i:s a',
strtotime("8/5/1992 12:30:06"));

 echo json_encode($e);
?>
```

Just execute the above code, and then observe what you get as the output. The output should be as follows:

{"name":"john","leisure":"sporting","birthdate":"08\
/05\/1992 12:30:06 pm"}

How to Decode JSON in PHP

The PHP function "json_decode()" can be used for the purpose of decoding JSON in PHP. This function will return a value which is decoded from JSON to the appropriate PHP type. It takes the syntax given below:

mixed json_decode ($json [,$assoc = false [, $depth = 512 [, $options = 0]]])

The following parameters have been used:

• json_string – this is an encoded string that must be a UTF-8 encoded data.

• assoc – this is a boolean type parameter, that after being set to TRUE, the returned objects will be converted to associative arrays.

- depth – this is an integer type parameter that specifies the recursion depth.
- options – this is an integer type bitmask of a JSON decode, JSON_BIGINT_AS_STRING is supported.

Consider the example given below which shows how one can use PHP to decode JSON objects:

```php
<?php
  $json = '{"p":1,"q":2,"r":3,"s":4,"t":5}';
  var_dump(json_decode($json));
  var_dump(json_decode($json, true));
?>
```

After execution of the above code, we will get the result shown below:

```
object(stdClass)#1 (5) {
  ["p"] => int(1)
  ["q"] => int(2)
  ["r"] => int(3)
  ["s"] => int(4)
  ["t"] => int(5)
}
array(5) {
  ["p"] => int(1)
  ["q"] => int(2)
  ["r"] => int(3)
  ["s"] => int(4)
  ["t"] => int(5)
}
```

Chapter 10- JSON with Perl

In this chapter, you will be guided on how to decode and encode JSON objects by the use of Perl programming language. The first step in this should involve setting up the environment for doing so.

Environment

The first thing should be installation of the JSON module. You can get this from CPAN. After downloading the latest version of this, follow the steps given below to install it:

$tar xvfz JSON-2.53.tar.gz
$cd JSON-2.53
$perl Makefile.PL
$make
$make install

JSON Functions

The following are the functions:
• encode_json- this function will convert the given Perl data structure into a binary string which is UTF-8 encoded.
• decode_json- this is used for decoding a JSON string.
• to_json-this is used for converting the given Perl data structure into a JSON string.
• from_json- this expects a JSON string and it then tries to parse it, to return the resulting reference.
• convert_blessed- this function is used with true value so that the method TO_JSON can be used by Perl on the class object for conversion of an object into JSON.

How to Encode JSON in Perl

The function "encode_json()" is used for conversion of a given Perl structure into a binary string which is UTF 8 encoded. It takes the syntax given below:

$json_text = encode_json ($perl_scalar);
or
$json_text = JSON->new->utf8-
>encode($perl_scalar);

Consider the example given below which shows arrays under JSON with Perl programming language:

```perl
#!/usr/bin/perl
use JSON;
my %rec_hash = ('p' => 1, 'q' => 2, 'r' => 3, 's' => 4, 't' => 5);
my $json = encode_json \%rec_hash;
print "$json\n";
```

Execution of the above code will give out the following result:

```
{"p":5,"q":3,"r":1,"s":2,"t":4}
```

To convert Perl objects into JSON, follow the example given below:

```perl
#!/usr/bin/perl
package Employee;
sub new {

  my $class = shift;

  my $self = {
    name => shift,
    leisure  => shift,
    birthdate  => shift,
  };

  bless $self, $class;
  return $self;
}

sub TO_JSON { return { %{ shift() } }; }
package main;

use JSON;
my $JSON = JSON->new->utf8;
$JSON->convert_blessed(1);
$emp = new Employee( "john", "sports", "8/5/1992 12:30:06 pm");
$json = $JSON->encode($emp);
print "$json\n";
```

After execution of the above code, you will get the following output:

{"birthdate":"8/5/1992 12:30:06 pm","name":"john","leisure":"sporting"}

How to Decode JSON into Perl

The function "decode_json()"in Perl can be used for the purpose of decoding JSON into Perl. When the method has been used, it will return the value which has been decoded from the JSON into the correct Perl. It takes the syntax given below:

$perl_scalar = decode_json $json_text
or
$perl_scalar = JSON->new->utf8->decode($json_text)

The example given below is a demonstration of how Perl can be used for the purpose of decoding JSON objects. In case you have not installed the module "Data::Dumper," then make sure that you install it. Here is the code:

```
#!/usr/bin/perl
use JSON;
use Data::Dumper;
$json = '{"p":1,"q":2,"r":3,"s":4,"t":5}';
$text = decode_json($json);
print  Dumper($text);
```

Execution of the above code will give you the following result:

```
$VAR1 = {
  'p' => 5,
  'q' => 3,

  'r' => 1,
  's' => 2,
  't' => 4
};
```

Chapter 11- JSON with Python

In this chapter, you will learn how to decode and encode JSON objects by use of Python programming language. Let us begin by setting up the environment so that we can get started.

Environment

Before beginning to encode and decode JSON by use of Python programming language, we should begin by installing the JSON modules which are available. In our case, we will use Demjson as shown below:

$tar xvfz demjson-1.6.tar.gz
$cd demjson-1.6
$python setup.py install

JSON Functions

- encode- this is used for encoding the Python object to a representation in JSON string .
- decode- this is used for decoding a JSON-encoded string into an object in Python.

Encoding (Encoding JSON into Python)

The Python function encode() is used for the purpose of encoding a Python object into a string represented in JSON. The syntax given below is used for doing this:

demjson.encode(self, obj, nest_level=0)
Consider the example given below of arrays under JSON using Python:

```
#!/usr/bin/python
import demjson
data = [ { 'p' : 1, 'q' : 2, 'r' : 3, 's' : 4, 't' : 5 } ]
json = demjson.encode(data)
print json
```
After execution of the above code, you will get the following output:

[{"p":1,"q":2,"r":3,"s":4,"t":5}]

The Python function "demjson.decode()" can be used for the purpose of decoding JSON. When this function has been used, it will return the Python type which has been decoded from the appropriate JSON type. It takes the syntax given below:

demjson.decode(self, txt)

Consider the example given below which shows how Python can be used for the purpose of decoding JSON objects. Here is the example:

```
#!/usr/bin/python
import demjson
json = '{"p":1,"q":2,"r":3,"s":4,"t":5}';
text = demjson.decode(json)
print text
```

Execution of the above code will give the following result:

{u'p': 1, u'r': 3, u'q': 2, u't': 5, u's': 4}

Chapter 12- JSON with Ruby

In this chapter, we will explore how to decode and encode JSON opens by use of Ruby programming language. The first thing should involve setting up the environment for working with Ruby and Python.

Environment

The first thing should involve installation of any JSON modules for Ruby which are currently available. If you are executing an older version of Ruby, you will have to make an installation of Ruby gem. However, if you are using the latest version of this, you may have the gem already installed, so you don't have to install it. My assumption is that you have gem already installed on your system. The next step should involve execution of the command given below:

$gem install json

How to parse JSON using Ruby

Consider the example given below in which the first two keys have been used for holding string values while the last three keys have been used for holding arrays of strings. Here is the example:

```
{
 "President": "Alan Juma",
 "CEO": "John Richardson",

 "USA": [
   "Sachin Joel",
   "Mercy Paul",
   "John Joel",
 ],

 "Srilanka": [
   "Lasith Smith",
   "Bosco Mathews",
   "Ken Oscar"
 ],
```

```
  "England": [
    "Alastair Obed",
    "Jonathan Mercy",
    "Kevin Jackson"
  ]

}
```

Below is a Ruby program which can be used for the purpose of parsing the above JSON document:

```
#!/usr/bin/ruby
require 'rubygems'
require 'json'
require 'pp'

json = File.read('input.json')
obj = JSON.parse(json)

pp obj
```

Execution of the above program will give you the following output:

```
{
  "President": "Alan Juma",
  "CEO": "John Richardson",
  "USA"=>
  [  "Sachin Joel", "Mercy Paul", "John Joel"],
  "Srilanka"=>
  ["Lasith Smith", "Bosco Mathews", "Ken Oscar"],
  "England"=>
  ["Alastair Obed", "Jonathan Mercy", "Kevin
Jackson"]
}
```

The names have been grouped according to their region as shown above.

Chapter 13- JSON with Java

It is possible for us to encode and decode JSON objects by use of the Java programming language. This book guides us on how to do this. Let us start be setting up our environment.

Environment

The first step before getting into the actual work is to install any of the JSON modules which are available. In this case, you can download and install the module JSON.simple. The location of the environment variable CLASSPATH should also be added.

How to map between JSON and Java Entities

The module JSON simple is used for mapping entities from the left side to your right side while parsing or decoding, and the entities are mapped from the right to the left during the process of encoding.

JSON can be encoded by use of Java. The example given below shows how JSON objects can be encoded using Java "*JSONObject.*" This is a subclass of the library "*java.util.HashMap.*" We have not provided any ordering. If you need performing strict ordering of the elements, you can make use of the method "JSONValue.toJSONString" with an implementation of an ordered map such as "java.util.LinkedHashMap." This is shown in the code given below:

```java
import org.json.simple.JSONObject;
class JsonEncodeDemo {
  public static void main(String[] args){
    JSONObject object = new JSONObject();
    object.put("name", "foo");
    object.put("num", new Integer(200));
    object.put("balance", new Double(2000.21));
    object.put("is_vip", new Boolean(true));
    System.out.print(object);
  }
}
```

Just compile and then execute the above program. You will observe the output given below:

{"balance": 2000.21, "num":200, "is_vip":true, "name":"foo"}

The code given below shows how the JSON "JSONObject" can be used for streaming a JSON object. Here is the code:

```
import org.json.simple.JSONObject;
class JsonEncodeDemo {
  public static void main(String[] args){
    JSONObject object = new JSONObject();
    object.put("name","foo");
    object.put("num",new Integer(200));
    object.put("balance",new Double(2000.21));
    object.put("is_vip",new Boolean(true));
    StringWriter out = new StringWriter();
    object.writeJSONString(out);
    String jText = out.toString();
    System.out.print(jText);
  }
}
```

Execution of the above code will give out the following output:

{"balance": 2000.21, "num":200, "is_vip":true, "name":"foo"}

How to Decode JSON in Java

In the example given below, we will use a *JSONObject* and *JSONArray*, in which *JSONArray* is a *java.util.List* while JSONObject is a *java.util.Map*.

Standard operations of list and map can be used for the purpose of accessing these. This is shown in the code given below:

```
import org.json.simple.parser.ParseException;
import org.json.simple.JSONObject;
import org.json.simple.parser.JSONParser;
import org.json.simple.JSONArray;
class JDecodeDemo {
  public static void main(String[] args){
        JSONParser parser = new JSONParser();
```

```java
        String string =
"[0,{\"1\":{\"2\":{\"3\":{\"4\":[5,{\"6\":7}]}}}}]";

        try{
          Object object = parser.parse(string);
          JSONArray array = (JSONArray)object;

          System.out.println("The 2nd element in our
array");
          System.out.println(array.get(1));
          System.out.println();

          JSONObject object2 = (JSONObject)array.get(1);
          System.out.println("Field \"1\"");
          System.out.println(object2.get("1"));

          singt = "{}";
          object = parser.parse(string);
          System.out.println(object);

          string = "[5,]";
          object = parser.parse(string);
          System.out.println(object);

          string = "[5,,2]";
          object = parser.parse(string);
          System.out.println(object);
        }catch(ParseException ex){

          System.out.println("position: " +
ex.getPosition());
          System.out.println(ex);
        }
      }
    }
}
```

Compilation and execution of the above program gives out the following output:

The 2nd element in our array
{"1":{"2":{"3":{"4":[5,{"6":7}]}}}}

Field "1"
{"2":{"3":{"4":[5,{"6":7}]}}}
{}
[5]
[5,2]

Chapter 14- JSON with Ajax

AJAX represents an asynchronous XML and JavaScript, and it is used for the purpose of web development on the client side as a group of related techniques, and we use it for development of asynchronous web applications. Based on the Ajax model, web applications can go sending and retrieving of data from the server asynchronously without the need of having to interfere with displaying and the existing web applications.

With most developers, JSON is used for the purpose of passing AJAX updates between the server and the client. A good example of Ajax is a website which updates live the scores of a sport. For the results to be posted on the website, you have to first store them in a server from which they will be retrieved. In this case, the behavior of the displayed page should not be affected. JSON formatted data can be used in this scenario.

Any data which has been updated by use of Ajax can be stored by use of JSON format on your web server. The use of Ajax is so that JavaScript can retrieve the JSON files when it becomes necessary, parse them, and then carry out the operations given below:

• Store the values which have been parsed into the variables so that they can be processed further before they can be displayed on the web page.

• The data will be directly assigned to the DOM elements in our web page, and this will make them able to be displayed on the website.

The code given below is an example of JSON with Ajax. Give the file a name with an "*.htm*" extension. The function "loadJSON()" has been used asynchronously for the purpose of uploading JSON data. The code is given below:

```
<html>
 <head>
   <meta content = "text/html; charset = ISO-8859-1"
http-equiv = "content-type">

   <script type = "application/javascript">
    function loadJSON(){
```

```javascript
        var data_file =
"http://www.mysite.com/json/data.json";
        var http_request = new XMLHttpRequest();
        try{
          // Opera 8.0+, Chrome, Firefox, Safari
          http_request = new XMLHttpRequest();
        }catch (ex){
          // Internet Explorer Browsers
          try{
            http_request = new
ActiveXObject("Msxml2.XMLHTTP");

          }catch (ex) {

            try{
              http_request = new
ActiveXObject("Microsoft.XMLHTTP");
            }catch (ex){
              // Something wrong happened
              alert("Your browser has broken down!");
              return false;
            }

          }
        }

        http_request.onreadystatechange = function(){

          if (http_request.readyState == 4 ){
            // Javascript function JSON.parse for
parsing JSON data
            var jObject =
JSON.parse(http_request.responseText);
            // jObject variable now has the data structure
and can
            // be accessed as a jObject.name and
jObject.country.
            document.getElementById("Name").innerH
TML = jObject.name;
```

```
        document.getElementById("Country").inner
HTML = jObject.country;
          }
        }

        http_request.open("GET", data_file, true);
        http_request.send();
      }
    </script>
    <title>mysite.com JSON</title>
  </head>

  <body>
    <h1> Details of Cricketer </h1>
    <table class = "src">
      <tr><th>Name</th><th>Country</th></tr>
      <tr><td><div id = "Name">John</div></td>
      <td><div id = "Country">USA</div></td></tr>
    </table>
    <div class = "central">
      <button type = "button" onclick =
"loadJSON()">Update Details </button>

    </div>
  </body>
</html>
```

You should have the input file which has the data in JSON format. This data will be uploaded after clicking on the button labelled *"Update Detail."* It is given below:

{"name": "mercy", "country": "Australia"}

Once you execute the program, click on the button, and then observe what happens.

Chapter 15- JSON Arrays

JSON arrays are used for representation of an ordered list of items. It can be used for storage of number, string, Boolean, or object in a JSON array. The values stored in the JSON array have to be separated by a comma. We need to demonstrate the different values which can be stored in a JSON array. These are discussed below:

A JSON array of numbers which is used for storage of numbers is given below:

[14, 25, 90, 67, 54]

A JSON array can also be used for storage of Boolean values. An example of this is given below:

[true, false, false, true, true]

A JSON array can also be used for the storage of objects. An example of this is given below:

{"students":[

   {"name":"John", "email":"john@gmail.com", "age": 26},

      {"name":"Mercy", "email":"mercy23@gmail.com", "age":18},

      {"name":"Joel", "email":"joel@gmail.com", "age":23},

      {"name":"Bob", "email":"bob32@gmail.com", "age":21}

   ]}

An array can also be stored inside another array in JSON. This is referred to as a multidimensional array pr an array of arrays.

An example of this is given below:

   [
   ["1", "2", "3"],
   ["p", "q", "r"],
   ["x", "y", "z"]
   ]

Chapter 16- JSONP

JSONP means JSON with padding. It is used for the purpose of requesting data which is located on a different domain. You might be asking the reason behind the need for a different technique to access the data. This is due to the Same Origin Policy.

The Same Origin Policy

The policy states that, if protocol (such as http), Port number (such as 80), and host (such as example.com) are different from where the data is being requested, it should not be permitted.

But the element "<script>" for HTML has to be allowed to retrieve content from foreign origins.

The functionality of JSONP

The first step should be creation of a callback function. The function will accept some data as the one shown below:

function callback(data){
console.log(data);
}

A script should then be included in a web page, and this should have the callback function which we created in the above step as a parameter. This is shown below:

<script
src="http://www.example.com?q=callback"><script>
This will output a script which will call the function, and the requested data is then passed. This is shown below:

callback({
"FirstName" : "joel",
"LastName" : "john",
"Grade" : "B"
}
);

JSONP and Ajax have nothing to do with each other, since the JSONP does not make use of XMLHttpRequest. Instead, it automatically inserts the tag "<script>" into the webpage. For

JQuery users who want to make use of this utility, you have to make use of the Ajax utility for JQuery. This is shown below:

```
$.ajax({
// ...
dataType: 'jsonp',

// ...
});
```

Where can JSONP be used?

JSONP is mostly used when we need to get data by use of RESTful APIs such as Flicker.
Consider the example given below:

```
<!DOCTYPE html>
<html>
<head>
<style>img{ height: 100px; float: left; }</style>
<script src="http://code.jquery.com/jquery-latest.js"></script>
<title>An JSONP sample from mysite</title>
/head>
<body>
<div id="images">
</div>
<script>
$.getJSON("http://api.flickr.com/services/feeds/photos_public.gne?jsoncallback=?",
{
tags: "dogs",
tagmode: "any",
format: "json"
},
function(data) {
$.each(data.items, function(j,item){
$("<img/>").attr("src",
item.media.m).appendTo("#images");
if ( j == 3 ) return false;
});
});</script>
```

```
</body>
</html>
```

In the above example, we are getting the latest updates from Flicker in regard to the tag "dogs" by use of both Ajax and JSONP.

json_last_error()

Consider the example given below:

```php
<?php $ json[] = "{'Website': 'mysite.com'}";
//now we have used "'" other than the double quote
(""), this is a syntax error.
foreach ($json as $ string) {
json_decode($string);
switch (json_last_error()) {
case JSON_ERROR_NONE:
echo ' - No errors';
break;
case JSON_ERROR_DEPTH:
echo ' - Maximum stack depth exceeded';
break;
case JSON_ERROR_STATE_MISMATCH:
echo ' – An Underflow or the modes have not
matched';
break;
case JSON_ERROR_CTRL_CHAR:
echo ' - Unexpected control character found';
break;
case JSON_ERROR_SYNTAX:
echo ' - Syntax error, malformed JSON';
break;
case JSON_ERROR_UTF8:
echo ' - Malformed UTF-8 characters, maybe due to
incorrect encoding';

break;
default:
echo ' - Unknown error';
break;
}
echo PHP_EOL;
```

```
}
?>
```

Nesting JSON Data

In case you have a large amount of data, you can store it in a nested format. One can choose to nest objects. An example of this is shown below:

```
var family = {
  "jason" : {
    "name" : "Joel John",
    "age" : "29",
    "gender" : "male"
  },
  "jackson" : {
    "name" : "Jackson John",
    "age" : "19",
    "gender" : "male"
  }
}
```

The nested arrays and JSON can be combined as we need, to store as many data as we need. The process of accessing data which has been stored in nested objects is very easy. The following snippet can be used for that purpose:

document.write(family.jason.name); // Output: Joel John
document.write(family.jackson.age); // Output: 19
document.write(family.joel.gender); // Output: male

Why JSON matters?

Currently, there are several Ajax-powered sites. This explains why there is a reason for us to create websites with the ability to load data more quickly and asynchronously. We also need to render the data in the background without the need of having to delay the rendering of the page. When we switch up the contents of a certain element within a layout without the need to refresh a page will add an amazing factor to our application. The users will also find it more convenient for them to use the app.

Social media has also become very popular in society today. Due to this, many other sites will highly rely on information that they get from Twitter, FaceBook, and other forms of social media. These sites usually provide us with RSS feeds which can be easily imported and used on the server-side, but for those who try to run these by use of Ajax, they will find it difficult. For an RSS feed to be used, it must be imported from the domain in which it is being stored. Consider an example in which we try to import the RSS feed for Flickr by use of the JQuery "*$.ajax()*" method. In this case, I get the JavaScript error given below:

[Exception... "Access to restricted URI denied" code: "1012"
nsresult: "0x805303f4
(NS_ERROR_DOM_BAD_URI)"

location:
"http://ajax.googleapis.com/ajax/libs/jquery/1.3.2/jquery.min.js Line: 19"]
A method named "*JSONP*" can be used in JSON to solve the cross-domain issue. This method makes use of a callback function for the purpose of sending the JSON data back to the domain. This functionality makes JSON very useful, and one finds it easy for them to carry out tasks which once seemed to be hard for them.

Loading JSON data into a Project

The Ajax method "*$.ajax()*" can be used for the purpose of loading JSON data into our web applications. This method is already available in our JQuery library. The ease with which data can be retrieved will vary depending on the site from which we are retrieving the data. Consider the simple example given below, which shows how this can be done:

```
$.ajax(
  type:'GET',
  url:"http://example.com/users/feeds/",
  data:"format=json&id=123",
  success:function(feed) {
    document.write(feed);
```

```
},
  dataType:'jsonp'
);
```

With the example given above, the latest feed items will be requested in a JSON format, and then they will be output in a browser. However, the example just shows how JSON can be used for loading data from an external source.

We need to demonstrate how to load Flickr streams by use of JQuery and Flickr. In this case, we will load photos only.

The first step should involve creation of the Ajax request. It is easy for us to access the Flickr's photostream feeds. Each of the user's possess a unique ID number, and this will be sent as part of the request to the URL. This is shown below:

http://api.flickr.com/services/feeds/photos_public.gne

The request which is to be sent will request the user for the latest photos, and the used flags will request the JSON-formatted response. The request should be sent as shown below:

id=XXX@NX&lang=en-us&format=json&jsoncallback=?

Note that in the code above, there are some parameters which have to be replaced with the user ID. We then want to create a function in which the user ID will be passed in as an argument. Let us create the function which will be used for the purpose of loading the JSON response. This is shown in the code given below:

```
function ldFlickr(flickrid)
{
  $('#feed').html('<span><img
src="/blog/images/lightbox-ico-loading.gif"
alt=""></span>');

  $.ajax({
    type:'GET',
    url:"http://api.flickr.com/services/feeds/photos_
public.gne",

    data:"id="+flickrid+"&lang=en-
us&format=json&jsoncallback=?",
```

```
    success:function(feed) {
        //Doing something on the response
    },
    dataType:'jsonp'
 });
}
```

The JSON data which will be returned will look as shown below:

"title": "Uploads from mydesign",

"link":
"http://www.flickr.com/photos/ennuidesign/",

"description": "",

"modified": "2015-12-17T04:53:38Z",

"generator": "http://www.flickr.com/",

"items": [

{

"title": "Do you need people to talk about you? This is
how you do it",

"link":
"http://www.flickr.com/photos/mydesign/336126925
1/",

"media":
{"m":"http://farm4.static.flickr.com/3470/33612692
51_9c55e6dc24_m.jpg"},

"date_taken": "2015-12-16T21:44:21-09:00",

"description": "<p><a href="http://www.flickr.com/people/mydesign/">my design</a> posted a photo:</p> <p><a title=" Do you need people to talk about you? This is how you do it " href="http://www.flickr.com/photos/mydesign/3361 269251/"><img src="http://farm4.static.flickr.com/3470/3361269251 _9c55e6dc24_m.jpg" alt=" Do you need people to talk about you? This is how you do it " width="240" height="180"></a></p> <p>I know of a guy, John Joel, who is an expert developer. He developed the website <a href="http://www.mysite.com/">for me</a> with his fellow developers, and te website looks very amazing to me and my customers.

 The design for the site is much good, including the colors which have been combined.

The frames themselves have been organized very well. The site loads quickly as compared to the ones my former developers had made for me. I recommend you to consult me if you need developing a site for your business. </p>",

"published": "2015-12-17T04:54:36Z",

"author": "somebody@flickr.com<script type="text/javascript">

/* <![CDATA[*/

(function(){try{var s,a,i,j,r,c,l=document.getElementById("__cf_email__");a=l.className;if(a){s='';r=parseInt(a.substr(0,2),16);for(j=2;a.length-j;j+=2){c=parseInt(a.substr(j,2),16)^r;s+=String.fromCharCode(c);}s=document.createTextNode(s);l.parentNode.replaceChild(s,l);}}catch(ex){}})();

/*]]> */

```
</script> (mydesign)",

"author_id": "29080075@N02",

"tags": "gift mydesign otherdesigns @designs"

}

// The rest of photos should be added here...

]

})
```

We need displaying the thumbnails of some of our images, and this will link us to the medium-sized image of the image. Flickr JSON is somehow confusing, but this will not provide us with a direct link to the photos in a thumbnail version. This means that we have to come up with a mechanism on our end to get to this, and this is what we are going to discuss. Each of the photo entries will have to be stored in an array, and Ajax will be used for the purpose of accessing this. For us to get data about each entry that is made, we will have to loop through the items to get to the last photo which we need.

The function should be modified, and then the loop setup as shown below:

function ldFlickr(flickrid)

{
// Displaying a loading icon for our display element

$('#feed').html('<img src="/blog/images/lightbox-ico-loading.gif" alt="">');

// Requesting the JSON and processing it

$.ajax({

type:'GET',

url: "http://api.flickr.com/services/feeds/photos_ public.gne",

data:"id="+flickrid+"&lang=en- us&format=json&jsoncallback=?",

```
success:function(feed) {

// Creating an empty array for storing images

var thumbs = [];

// Looping through our items

for(var j=0, l=feed.items.length; j < l && j <
16; j)

{

// Processing each image

}

// Displaying the thumbnails on our page

},

dataType:'jsonp'

});

}
```

We are only interested in the "*m*" element which has been stored in the "*media*" element. To access this within our loop, we can make use of "*feed.items[j].media.m*". A regular expression should then be executed on this value for the purpose of getting our thumbnail and image paths, and these will be assembled to get a linked thumbnail image. The HTML which has been assembled newly will then be put into the array of thumbs which we have created. Once we are through with looping, all the images will be combined into a single HTML string, and the contents of the displayed element will be replaced with the thumbnails which we have loaded. The code given below shows how this functionality can be added to our script:

```
function ldFlickr(flickrid)
{
  // Displaying the load icon in the display element
  $('#feed').html('<span><img
src="/blog/images/lightbox-ico-loading.gif"
alt=""></span>');

  // Requesting the JSON and then processing it
  $.ajax({
    type:'GET',
    url:"http://api.flickr.com/services/feeds/photos_
public.gne",
    data:"id="+flickrid+"&lang=en-
us&format=json&jsoncallback=?",

    success:function(feed) {
      // Creating an empty array for storing images
      var thumbs = [];
      // Looping through our items
      for(var j=0, l=feed.items.length; j < l && j < 16;
  i)
      {
        // Manipulating the image to get thumb and
the medium sizes

        var image = feed.items[j].media.m.replace(
        /^(.*?)_m.jpg$/,
        '<a href="/blog/$img.jpg"><img
src="/blog/$img2.jpg" alt=""></a>'

        );
        // Adding the new element to our array
        thumbs.push(image);
      }
      // Displaying the thumbnails on our page
      $('#feed').html(thumbs.join(''));
```

```
    // A function for adding a lightbox effect
    addLB();
  },
  dataType:'jsonp'
});
}
```
The light box effect has also been added to our thumbnails due to the use of the function "*addLB()*" to our code. This good for making it fun.

Conclusion

It can be concluded that JSON is a very useful standard when it comes to development of web applications. Most people need transmitting data in a format which is readable by humans. JSON is an open standard which can assist people in doing this. It provides the developers with an easy to do mechanism on how the data which they need to transmit can be done in a human-readable format. In some situations, there might be a need for you to live update the data in your website. A good example is when there is a sporting match. This can be done by use of JSON. This shows how the standard is useful to the programming community.

The good thing about JSON is that it can be used with the various programming languages which are available today for the purpose of creating applications. Examples of these programming languages include Perl, Java, PHP, and Scala. In cases where you want to connect JSON to any of these environments, you have to begin by setting up the environment so that they can work together.

This always involves the installation of the necessary JSON modules which are available for each of these programming languages. It is after setting up these that you can get into the actual programming. My hope is that this book has helped you understand the core concepts of JSON!

Printed in Great Britain
by Amazon

34757344R00036